Words *for* Cards

A Collection

500 engaging quotables for those countless
occasions of when you've got the right card,
but can't find the right words

"Words For Cards"
By Bruce Hultgren
ISBN No. 978-0-9871106-0-2

First Published 2011 by Bruce Hultgren
www.facebook.com/wordsforcards
www.facebook.com/pocketangels
www.pocketangels.com

ISBN 978-0-9871106-0-2

Publisher: Bruce Hultgren
Project Editor: Belinda Hultgren
Cover Design: Blucanvis Branding
www.facebook.com/BlucanvisBranding

Dedication:

Belinda, Conner & Jamieson
"When I Think Of You I Smile"

Contents

Anniversary

The day we got married was the
proudest of my life.
Happy Anniversary.

Every Anniversary is special. A
Golden one, filled with memories,
caring and love is simply amazing.
Sincerest Congratulations
to you both.

The essence of love is eternal.

If only everyone could be so
lucky as you/us.

You know you're blessed when
you radiate love like you both do.
Congratulations.

You know how much I love
bacon? Well, I love you
more than that!

Thank you for still looking at me
and giving me butterflies –
I love you.

I love you more than you
will ever know.

To share each other and what
each other loves, it's wonderful to
see you accomplish
this each day.
Congratulations on the
love you share.

I am so lucky and proud to have
someone as loving and
amazing as you.
Happy Anniversary.

To the couple who were
definitely made for each other.
Happy Anniversary.

Together forever,
whatever the weather.

How blessed you are to
remember that feeling you first
got when you realized you
wanted this to last forever...
actually will.
Happy Anniversary.

I can't count the number
of times I've fallen in
love with you all over again.
Thank You.
Happy Anniversary.

On this day and every day...
I give you my heart.

Ten/Five etc... Years ago you
committed to your relationship
and your love for one another.
Be very proud that you can
celebrate this day together
because of the strength of the
love you share.

All because two people
fell in love.

Your story.
Once upon a time.....
and they lived happily
ever after.
Congratulations.

To my life partner, I love you...
for what, and who you are, and
for what I am when I'm with you.

If I could have described the
perfect person to be my loving
companion and best friend, I
would have described you.

2 Apology

I wanted to have the last word.....
SORRY.

* * * * * * * *

Seeing you hurting is harder than
me admitting I'm wrong.
I'm sorry.

* * * * * * * *

I want to kiss and make up
because I was wrong and I'm
sorry. Please forgive me.

* * * * * * * *

I'm not going to have peace until
you forgive me for the hurt I've
caused you. I'm so sorry.

* * * * * * * *

You needed a shoulder to cry on
and someone to talk to.
Sorry I wasn't there for you.

Please forgive me for the words I
said but did not mean. Know that
when I say sorry I mean it.

* * * * * * * *

I want to mend our friendship and
be a better friend. Sorry to put you
through such a hard time.

* * * * * * * *

I love you for your forgiving nature,
your understanding and for you.
Thank you.

* * * * * * * *

Nothing would be too hard or too
much to accomplish if it meant
I would have your love and
forgiveness for the damage I have
done, I'm sorry.

* * * * * * * *

Please tell me we are not beyond
repair. I'm so sorry and I hope it's
not too late.

You were right, I was wrong….
Sorry.

Apologies should never contain
an excuse. I'm just sorry.

Sometimes the magic word isn't
"please" – it's "sorry". Please
accept this magic word from me.

If I didn't bruise so easily I'd
let you sock me one!

The gracious gift of an apology
can sometimes be just the gift
you need. Please accept mine.

Sorry I've been such a…
you know what!

You lose sixty seconds of
happiness for every minute
you're angry. Sorry for taking
away your happiness time.

Sorry I made your day
less than wonderful.

I can't begin to tell you enough,
just how sorry I am.

Words should always be soft and
tender in case you ever have to
eat them. Got sauce?

3 Birthdays

My eyes twinkle at the
thought of you.

* * * * * * * *

Today is YOUR special day to
shine, Happy Birthday to YOU.

* * * * * * * *

When I think of you I smile.

* * * * * * * *

May today and everyday be a
celebration of YOU.

* * * * * * * *

As your god parent, I promise to
guide and protect you.
I am so proud that
you're in my life.

May today be a reflection of
the many days to come that we
celebrate you in the world.

* * * * * * * *

You brighten up our days with
your twinkling eyes and
sparkling smile.

* * * * * * * *

The pride and feelings we
have for you, simply cannot be
expressed – we love you.

* * * * * * * *

You are so special and unique,
that there is no one in the world
just like you.

* * * * * * * *

When you look in the mirror, see
how special you are, we love you
for you!

May this be the best Birthday
ever. Hope there's lots of
fun and laughter.

There are 1440 minutes in a day
– on your Birthday – we hope you
enjoy every single
one of them.

On this day the world became a
better place because
you arrived.

Looks like another chance to
build on the expression...
"The older I get the better I was!"
Happy Birthday... you legend!

Sometimes words can't express
just how much you mean to me.
Happy, Happy Birthday.

Hoping your day makes your face
hurt from smiling too much.

Happy Birthday to the
sunshine in our lives.
Happy Birthday to the most
thoughtful and gentle
person we know.

May all the wishes you make
today come true for you.

For my friend who lights up the
room, go ahead and wish for the
stars – you deserve it.

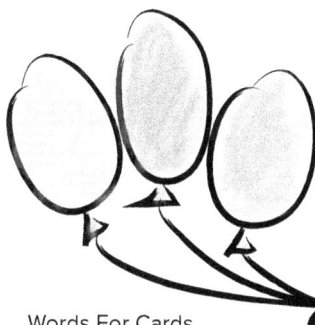

Sending you lots of love for
your special day.

4 Bon Voyage

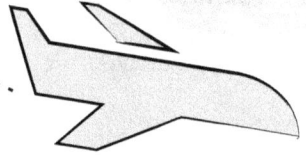

I've never liked goodbye's so to you I say farewell.

* * * * * * * *

I'm going to miss you more than you could know.

* * * * * * * *

Travel safely on your journey, take in the sights and sounds. Then come back safely to us, and tell us stories that will astound.

* * * * * * * *

Today we say Goodbye. Not forever, just for a while.

* * * * * * * *

You know I am going to miss you. Your laugh, your smile, your eyes.

May your trip be the best ever.

* * * * * * * *

Have a wonderful trip that will create lots of amazing memories.

* * * * * * * *

Please don't be gone too long, we'll miss you.

* * * * * * * *

Life is a voyage – enjoy every single moment of your journey.

* * * * * * * *

Miles may come between us, but our thoughts will be with you there.

As you depart to see new horizons, know that we'll miss you while you're gone.

A kind kiss, a dropping tear before we part, but I'll see you soon. Bon Voyage.

You and I will meet again someday soon. I'm looking forward to it already.

It's not just "Happy Trails" – it's the way you ride those trails. Enjoy every minute.

Sweet will be my memory of my soon to be distant friend. I'll miss you.

A farewell is necessary before we can meet again.

I'm lucky because saying goodbye to you is so hard.

Do whatever makes you happy. Enjoy the journey, travel safely.

Your melody will linger on, long after the song has finished.

Keep a map of home close to your heart as you go on your journey. Bon Voyage.

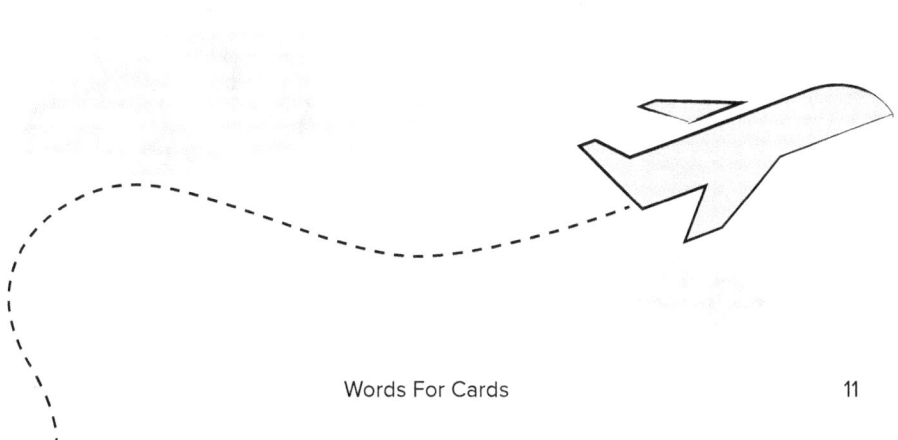

5

Christening

May your Guardian Angel watch
over you, protect you and guide
you as you grow.

* * * * * * * *

We look forward to watching you
grow into a very special person
from this day forwards.

* * * * * * * *

What a wonderful,
special, miracle you are.

* * * * * * * *

Thanks for allowing us to share
this most special of days.

* * * * * * * *

May all the beauty and happiness
in the world come knocking
on your door.

We celebrate you...
beautiful child.

* * * * * * * *

You are living proof that
Angels exist.

* * * * * * * *

Thank you for letting us share this
most special of events with you.

* * * * * * * *

May your sense of wonder you
experience as a child, stay with
you your whole life.

* * * * * * * *

May your life be filled with
"doing things for the first time".

The world is at your fingertips.

Catch this moment and put it in
your heart forever.

This will be one of the precious
moments we cherish.

Today is just so special
in every way.

From Heaven's brightest star, we
celebrate the gift of an Angel.

Beautiful child...
Welcome to the world.

Congratulations to our dear
friends on this memorable event.

A baby is the sweetest
blessing of them all.

You are living proof that dreams
really do come true.

If I could wish for the perfect
dream for you, I'd wish you got
the parents you did.

6 Christmas

May the Christmas Spirit
fill your home this Season.

* * * * * * *

It's Christmas, I'm feeling
"Santamental".

* * * * * * *

May the memories of this
Christmas stay with you forever.

* * * * * * *

Everything is softer and more
beautiful when Christmas waves
a magic wand over the world.

* * * * * * *

With thoughts of a bright shining
star on a silent night, a world full
of peace, hope and joy – these I
wish for you. Merry Christmas.

* * * * * * *

Christmas…
makes everything beautiful.

* * * * * * *

With Christmas comes love,
friendship and joy –
I wish all these for you.

* * * * * * *

I wish you a merry "Kissmas".

* * * * * * *

Be sure to take time to stop,
breath and take in all the
wonders of the Season.

May the feeling of Christmas
be with you all year.

The sound you hear in the room when presents are being opened is Love.

Christmas can only fill the air if at first it fills our hearts.

Christmas is in your heart, not under a tree.

Christmas is one of the only appointments kept by man over the centuries.

May your Christmas morning be filled with…
"No Assembly Required"

May all roads lead to home this Christmas.

Don't clean up the mess created on Christmas morning too quickly – it's a mess to behold!

Give your love, give your time, give you, so the recipient will feel like it's Christmas no matter what day it is.

Live Christmas every day and wish for peace on earth.

The state of mind that is Christmas, may it find you each day you awake to start each day.

7 Congratulations On your...

Home... Where lifetime memories are created every day. Congratulations.

* * * * * * * *

Beautiful people turn a house into a beautiful home. Congratulations.

* * * * * * * *

It was only a matter of time before you were recognized for your hard work. Congratulations.

* * * * * * * *

Welcome to a new chapter in your life. Enjoy every page.

* * * * * * * *

May your smile lines grow deep from the joy this new adventure brings to you.

Always remember to have fun on the journey.

* * * * * * * *

Today is the first day of your future – enjoy it!

* * * * * * * *

If you love what you do, you'll never work a day in your life.

* * * * * * * *

On the door of Opportunity – the sign says... PUSH!

* * * * * * * *

The door to a new beginning is open for you to go through. Enjoy it! Congratulations.

For someone who desires to achieve – nothing will stop them.

Think of this new opportunity as your chance to change the world. Congratulations.

Congratulations on getting your license. Don't Drive faster than your Guardian Angel can fly!

To complete is not the end, it's the beginning.

You've passed with flying colors, We're/I'm very proud of you.

I am very proud of you.

A whole new world is yours now that you've passed your test – Congratulations.

Congratulations on making the effort to change your situation.

We all have the power to make a new tomorrow through our talents, dreams and destinations.

Congratulations on your ability to make others happy – it is a gift that I'm pleased you shared with me.

8 Education - Exams, Graduation

The time has come to celebrate
The day on which you graduate –
Sincerest Congratulations.

* * * * * * * *

One of life's journeys is being
tested and passing.
You've done that with flying
colors, Congratulations.

* * * * * * * *

Good luck on your exams.
It's time for you to shine.
With clarity, focus and
piece of mind.

* * * * * * * *

There's an Angel
watching over you,
Protecting you and your dreams.
Go forth, be strong,
enjoy the journey.

* * * * * * * *

Congratulations on passing,
your work has paid off.

Your dedication to the task over
a period of time has bought
outstanding results. May your
new journey take you to where
your dreams will be fulfilled.

* * * * * * * *

Achievement = you passing
and following your dreams.
Congratulations.

* * * * * * * *

To accomplish great things
we must dream.
Good luck on your exams.

* * * * * * * *

Be courageous,
Be calm, Go Conquer.
Good luck on your exams.

* * * * * * * *

Not once was there
any doubt you'd graduate –
Congratulations.

May the many doors to success that await you be easily opened as a result of you getting your degree. Congratulations.

Con – GRAD – ulations!

To new beginnings because of happy endings. Congratulations.

With an open heart, a brilliant mind and knowledge in your head. Success is anything you want it to be.

Embrace the infinite world of possibilities that now await your arrival. Congratulations.

Whatever your dreams may be, may this be the first single step towards them. Congratulations.

Shine brightly, reach far, dream big. Congratulations.

Hold your memories in one hand and leave the other one open to catch your dreams.

I can hear the calls for the celebration of celebrations to commence. Congratulations.

Go confidently in the pursuit of your dreams. You can do anything.

Friendship

Please know that I'm here for
you, anytime, anywhere.
As you would be for me.

Thank you for being my friend.

Carry these words with you and
when you feel the need,
know that someone cares.

You were there when I needed
you and I'll never forget that.

Guidance, Strength, Love –
you bring these to my life.
I cherish our friendship and I say.
Thank You.

When I needed someone,
you were there.

A true friend who
can never be replaced.

Our friendship is as
valuable as treasure.
To be able to call you friend –
is one of life's great pleasures.

For you my friend,
the gift of the written word.
To let you know that I Love You
and Cherish our friendship.

The friendship that we
share is a special gift.
I'll cherish it forever.

You've made a footprint on my
heart that will be there forever.
Thank You.

Diamonds are as rare as a
friendship such as ours.

Our lives are connected
because you cared.

You didn't tell me
what I wanted to hear,
you told me the way it was.
Thanks for keeping it honest.

You helped ease
my pain in my
time of sorrow –
Thank you.

Your strength is appreciated
during this time.

You're not family –
I'm glad I chose you to
be a part of my life.

You....World =
Happier, Better.

You've encouraged me,
supported me and overlooked
my weaknesses.
A true friend you really are.

Because of you
I believe in
real life Angels.

10 Get Well

May you feel the strength of
the many who are on
this journey with you.

* * * * * * * *

Don't ever feel
alone on this journey.
There are many who will help you
and support you.

* * * * * * * *

Sometime words are not enough,
but you're always on my mind.
Know that you are in my thoughts.
And I wish you love and strength.

* * * * * * * *

Like a flower... no, a rose
You brighten up the
world just by being you –
You are missed,
please get well soon.

* * * * * * * *

May your journey against this
illness, be a battle you will win.

I heard the news of your
battle with an illness,
I wish you Love, Strength and
Light on your journey.

* * * * * * * *

There's an Angel
watching over you
To protect, comfort
and guide you.

* * * * * * * *

I wish you luck on
this journey to health.

* * * * * * * *

May the friendship and love of
many be your greatest
healing therapy.

* * * * * * * *

It's not the same without you.
We're looking forward to seeing
your smile, and the renewed
strength your happiness will
bring. Get Well Soon.

Enjoy being cared for,
you deserve it.

Enjoy the remote
while you recover.

Getting back to work is harder
than getting back to health!
Take your time and get well soon.

May the sun shine upon you so
you won't be feeling
under the weather.
Get Well Soon.

From my heart I send you
strength, love and good wishes.

There's a vacuum since you've
been gone. Come back soon and
show us how to work it!

You're always so generous,
it's our turn to take care of you.

We said a prayer for you today.

I was going to cook you
something, but then I figured,
why make it worse? It would
probably "taste like chicken" no
matter what I made anyway!!!!

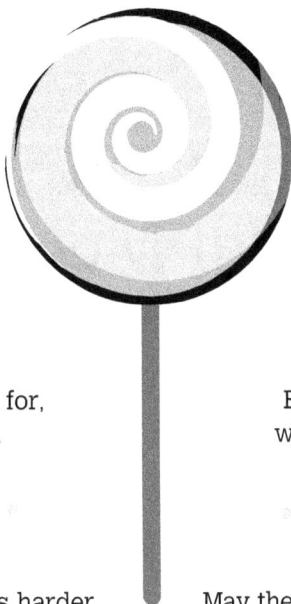

Why is it that you can read
a Doctors bill but not his
handwriting?

11 Good Luck, Farewell, New Job, We'll Miss You

Good Luck, Farewell,
We'll Miss You.
We'll count the minutes and days
until you return safely to us.

· · · · · · · ·

You are surrounded by Angels.

· · · · · · · ·

You're off to celebrate
a fresh and brand new start
May every step towards your
dream lift you higher.

· · · · · · · ·

Go forwards with a purpose,
and may your goals be
all you dream of.

· · · · · · · ·

Good luck on your new venture,
you'll be missed.

Sorry to see you leaving, please
keep in touch – I'm on Facebook!

· · · · · · · ·

Things just won't be the same
when you're not around.

· · · · · · · ·

Knowing I was going to
see you at work made
my days so enjoyable.

· · · · · · · ·

Can I come?

· · · · · · · ·

I can honestly say that a true
highlight in my life has been
getting to know you
Let's keep in touch.

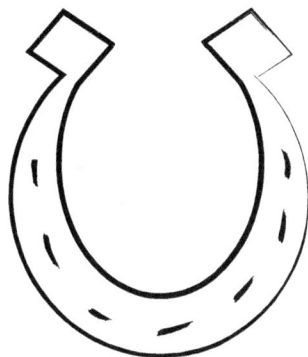

I'll say farewell instead of
goodbye because we
will meet again soon.

Our true emotions are always
presented in the hour of
farewell and of greeting.

I am sad to say goodbye, but
someone is about to meet you
and get to know you like me.
I wish I could do
that all over again.

Isn't it strange that goodbyes can
take forever but the hello
was but a moment.

There's a very special moment,
just one moment, when the door
opens and lets the future in.
Good Luck.

May the Angels light
the path for you.

Wishing you the best of luck.

May your cookies
be full of good fortune.

It is said the greatest thing in
the world is the direction we're
moving, not where we are now.
Congratulations.

This is your time to change
the world. Go For It.
We'll miss you.

Happiness Quotes

Enjoy the day -
it is a one of a kind!

* * * * * * * *

Without Adventure, there can be
NO Life Changing Experiences!

* * * * * * * *

Unless you have FUN in what
you are doing - you will very
likely not succeed!

* * * * * * * *

Take 4 minutes right now to
stop the outside noise, relax,
breathe and appreciate what
you have the ability to do.

* * * * * * * *

Live deliberately -
with intention and purpose.

Have you ever noticed....
the best swimmers are
always in the pool.

* * * * * * * *

Become the most positive and
enthusiastic person you know.

* * * * * * * *

As of today (and everyday) -
you have 100% of your life left -
use it wisely!!!!

* * * * * * * *

Think big thoughts,
but relish small pleasures.

* * * * * * * *

Make it a habit to do nice things
for people who'll never find out.

Smile a LOT. It costs nothing
and is beyond price.

Mistakes ARE LIFE!
They are not to be tolerated...
they are to be ENCOURAGED!

"Get Your Priorities Straight!"
Have you even seen
a headstone that said...
"Wished I'd spent more
time at the office".

You'll NEVER get to WOW unless
you are at least willing
to aspire to it!

PLAY.

Is there any reason for you not to
do something nice for someone
less fortunate than you today?

Let Everyone Talk!

Make The World A Better Place.

Don't Rust Out.....
WEAR Out!

Live your life so that your
epitaph could read......
"No Regrets".

13 ◆ Inspirational

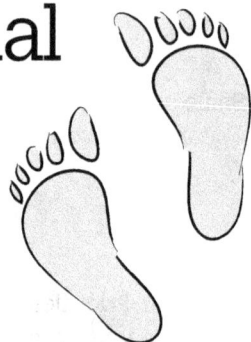

You inspire me with
your commitment.
May all your dreams come true.

* * * * * * * *

As you make your
way on this journey
May the universe shine
upon you and light the way.

* * * * * * * *

Tomorrow is going
to be amazing for you.
Everyone who sees you
says the same thing –
Go For It.

* * * * * * * *

You make a difference with every
step and breath you take.
We're amazed at you and how
unique you are.

* * * * * * * *

My friend, you've touched my life
and I will never be the same.

When I see the stars in the sky,
I think of you.

* * * * * * * *

I'll never take you for granted,
I realize you're a diamond.

* * * * * * * *

New Day...
New Beginnings.

* * * * * * * *

May you live each day so
your memories will create
your happiness.

* * * * * * * *

Because there are footprints
on the moon, I know
anything is possible.

Only when you take time
to focus on your dreams will
they come into focus.

It's only a mistake if we don't
learn from it – otherwise, it's
just a learning opportunity.

This life is all about you –
don't spend time living
someone else's dream.

The shadows will fall behind you
when you turn to face the sun.

Don't make time to relax...
just do it now!

Many things seemed impossible...
until they weren't.

Education is not something to do
before you commence your life,
it is an integral part of it.

Dare... to be YOU!

Where there is an absence of fear
– you will find courage.

If you believe...
you can achieve...
anything.

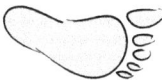

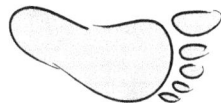

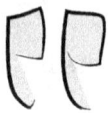

14 Inspirational Quotes

(Life Tips)

NEVER give up on anybody.
Miracles happen every day.

* * * * * * * *

Live today like it is your last -
for one day -
you will be right!!!!

* * * * * * * *

It is not failing that is
unacceptable -
it is not trying.

* * * * * * * *

May today be the BEST first day
of the rest of your life!

* * * * * * * *

Follow Your Dreams
Every Day.

"Don't Expect Others To Listen
To Your Advice And
Ignore Your Example."

* * * * * * * *

What can you celebrate about
this week - what little victories
did you have?

* * * * * * * *

Keep It Simple.

* * * * * * * *

When complimented, a sincere
"Thank You" is the ONLY
response required.

* * * * * * * *

Hard to learn -
easy to teach - pass it on!

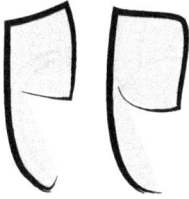

You don't drown by falling in the water, you drown by staying there!

Hug Someone.

Everyday day above ground is a good day.

Be Your Partner's Best Friend.

It isn't the mountain ahead that wears you out...
It is the grain of sand in your shoe!

WHY NOT wish for a magnificent life of complete fulfillment?
WHY NOT devote your full energy to attaining the goals you set?

Evaluate yourself by your own standards, NOT someone else's!

Call Your Mother!

Wear Your Passion On Your Sleeve. People Sign Up To Follow Passionate Leaders!

There is NO wind...........
ROW!!!!!

15 ◆ Love

I can't help it – I Love You and I smile when I think of you.

⦿ ⦿ ⦿ ⦿ ⦿ ⦿ ⦿ ⦿

Thank You for making me a part of your life's journey.

⦿ ⦿ ⦿ ⦿ ⦿ ⦿ ⦿ ⦿

It's you I love,
for you live within me.
In secret, untouchable places.

⦿ ⦿ ⦿ ⦿ ⦿ ⦿ ⦿ ⦿

In my life's biography,
you're on every line.

⦿ ⦿ ⦿ ⦿ ⦿ ⦿ ⦿ ⦿

A river cannot wash the love I feel for you, you're the seal on my heart.

I said a prayer for you today, that you're with me for all my life.

⦿ ⦿ ⦿ ⦿ ⦿ ⦿ ⦿ ⦿

A view shared with you
is simply priceless.

⦿ ⦿ ⦿ ⦿ ⦿ ⦿ ⦿ ⦿

On any given day, my perfect day begins with you.

⦿ ⦿ ⦿ ⦿ ⦿ ⦿ ⦿ ⦿

Thankfully I don't remember what life was like before you captured my heart.

⦿ ⦿ ⦿ ⦿ ⦿ ⦿ ⦿ ⦿

I Love YOU, all of you, always will. Yes – you have all of me.

You're filling my life with moments that take my breath away. Thank You.

"I dreamed a dream that I would find the "you and me" that we have. Thanks for being my best friend and lover. I cherish every day.

I said a prayer for you today.

The look in your eyes that is saved for only me, is something I cherish each time I see it. Everything is possible when I see the love in your smile.
I love you.

You were on my mind today..... again!

Everything is possible when I see the love in your smile.
I love you.

You and I have what single people are searching for around the world. Wow!

Somebody in this world loves you, needs you, is proud of you, can't wait to see you, thinks the world of you, would die for you, and most of all, thinks you are the perfect partner.
Thank you for being you.

To be together forever is what I'm counting down to everyday that you're away from me.

I no longer have shadows around me because your love shines so brightly on my life.

16 Missing You

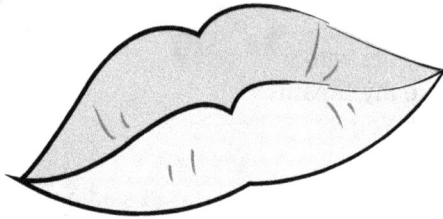

The day they are hollow,
the sun, it doesn't shine.
I miss you every single day
But I smile when you
come to mind.

* * * * * * * *

I miss your smile, because when
you smile, you mean it.

* * * * * * * *

Wish you were here.

* * * * * * * *

I miss hearing your voice.

* * * * * * * *

I miss laughing with you.

I miss that "instant vacation"
which is laughing with you.

* * * * * * * *

Every day I wish for you.

* * * * * * * *

Thinking of you...
and chocolate!

* * * * * * * *

I miss your smiley face.

* * * * * * * *

Two souls, one heart, miss you.

Kindness and love will always
make a difference.
Miss You.

A good friend is
cheaper than therapy!
Miss you.

Your friendship isn't a big thing,
it's a million little things.

Goodnight....
Wherever you are.

When you look into the sky from
where you are, and I look
into the sky where I am,
we can be connected.
Miss You.

The days I miss you the most
are... those that end in "y".

Sending you love no matter
where you are.

You are beautiful and unique
and I miss you.

Just thought I'd check to see
how you're going.
Miss You.

You shared your happiness seed
with me and it became a flower,
Thank You, Miss You!

17 Mother or Father Birthday

What a wonderful gift your
parents gave the world
on this day.

* * * * * * * *

You are my hero
And I'm proud to call you Dad.

* * * * * * * *

Today is a day that we can
celebrate you and all
you've achieved.

* * * * * * * *

If I could bottle up the pride
I have about you,
They couldn't make a lid strong
enough to hold it all in.

* * * * * * * *

Yes! You made me what I am
today! Happy Birthday!

* * * * * * * *

Ever since I placed my tiny hand
in yours, I've loved you more
than I can express.

* * * * * * * *

It's time for me to say
"I'm very proud of you"
Love you always –
Happy Birthday.

* * * * * * * *

Sometimes we want to
forget Birthdays.
Let's celebrate what
you've achieved.

* * * * * * * *

I want you to know that I
appreciate every single thing
you've done for me. Thank you
for making me a part of your
life. I hope I leave the same
impression on my children.
Happy Birthday with
Respect & Love.

The world is simply a better place
because you're in it.

May today be the first day of the rest of your life! Happy Birthday.

Whenever I look up to the warm sun – I think of you. Thank you for all you've done. Lots of Love on your Birthday.

On this glorious day we celebrate your love, your friendship and your life. Happy Birthday.

To dream, to set another goal, there is never a bad age. Go For It.

The trick for you now is this... to grow up without getting old.

The secret to youthful looking skin is tricking your mind that your birthday is a certain number without your body finding out.

You do know the best birthdays are yet to come... right? Enjoy each and every one.

The difference between men and women. Women won't admit their age while men won't act it!

Enjoy the process of ageing, many simply don't get to experience it.

Beautiful is a perfect word that comes to mind when I think of you and your Birthday. May it be everything you dream of.

18 ◆ Mother's or Father's Day

#1 DAD

Thank you for loving me, understanding me and encouraging me for as long as I can remember.

For being there, for supporting me, for being my cheer squad, Thank You.

All my life I'll be grateful for you.

Because I have you... my world is a better place.

Three words can let you know how much I appreciate you....
I Love You.

I hope you're as proud of me as I am of you.

Thanks for making me what I am today.

Thanks for your patience during my formative years.
I don't know how you did it!!!
Is it too late to say sorry?

Because you deserve the absolute best....
You got me!

I am where I am today because of your influence on my life –
Thank you.

How is it that you know exactly what to say, no matter when I call? Thank You.

You've inspired me through your compassion, your love and your beautiful nature. You've taught me so much. Thank You.

You've given me the courage and inspiration to face my fears and find my own success. For that... I thank you.

Sorry it took so long for me to appreciate what you did for me. Now that I'm a parent... I get it. Thank You for all you did and continue to do for my life.

Thank you for your love, patience and guidance so I could build my strength and independence.

Although I didn't always agree with you, I now see your wisdom through your guidance and love. Thanks for making me learn those lessons.

I can conquer the world because of you.

Thank you for helping all my dreams come true.

I am proud to call the most important person in my life my Mother/Father.

No matter my height, I will always look up to you.

#1 MOTHER

19 New Baby Or Pregnancy

Sincerest Congratulations on
the arrival of your new baby.
You'll wonder what you
ever did without them.

* * * * * * * *

A brand new little person
is on the way,
Enjoy the journey you're taking
and cherish every day.

* * * * * * * *

An Angel sent from up
above is what you are.
Perfect in every single way –
welcome to the world.

* * * * * * * *

May all the colors, sights and
sounds of your days
create a lifelong memory for you.

* * * * * * * *

Just like a baby, we never
outgrow the need to be loved.
Congratulations.

Life is about to get much,
much better – I guarantee it.
Congratulations.

* * * * * * * *

You are destined to grow into an
amazing person because you'll
take after your parents.
Welcome to the world.

* * * * * * * *

There is no greater moment in
time as that when your baby
first looks into your eyes and
takes hold of your finger.
Congratulations.

* * * * * * * *

The first smile, the thousands
of hours of just staring and
laughing, is the beginning of
a magical lifelong journey.
Congratulations.

* * * * * * * *

I bet you didn't even know
you had this amount of love in
you for this brand new person.
Amazing isn't it?

A baby means that your days ahead are going to be filled with love, happiness, smiles and cherished memories. Congratulations.

As you hold your baby in your arms, savour the miracle of life and the power entrusted to you. You will be amazing parents.

And the saying goes….
"A Star Is Born" –
Congratulations.

Hey Baby!
Welcome to the world little one!

Goonee goo goo –
a world of baby talk awaits.
Congratulations.

A baby is living proof that you can live while your heart is on the outside. Congratulations.

To share a quiet moment with your baby is priceless, enjoy each and every one of them.

To look into your babies eyes and say I love you without saying a word is nothing short of amazing.

Watching your new baby sleep and taking a moment to think about all that this world has to offer is quite extraordinary – be sure to take in all these moments as they happen. Document them and take lots of photo's. You'll be glad you did.

Take more photos of every moment you can, these moments in time can never be repeated. Congratulations.

20 Retirement

Your Monday mornings will never
be looked at the same.
Enjoy them!

* * * * * * * *

You've earned this "start of
something new" – enjoy it.

* * * * * * * *

You have touched and influenced
so many during your time
here. Sincerest Thanks and
Congratulations.

* * * * * * * *

All you have achieved here
will never be forgotten.
Thank You and Congratulations.

* * * * * * * *

The happiness in the anticipation
of a brand new day is wished for
you every day.
Congratulations.

The door to a new beginning has
been opened exclusively for you.

* * * * * * * *

A new day,
a new adventure, enjoy...

* * * * * * * *

Please come back and visit.
You'll be so missed.

* * * * * * * *

The key to our success has been
the person you see in the mirror
each day. Thank you so much.

* * * * * * * *

I hope that one day I can be
blessed to again work with
someone just as unique as you.

The challenge of spending time
without spending money
awaits you.... Enjoy!!!

If you're ever wondering if you
left a footprint anywhere – look
no further than right here.
Thank you.

Your future is bright with dreams
to aspire to. My best wishes
travel with you.

You've got a brand new book
and the pages are blank, ready
for you to write some brand new
stories into it. Enjoy the journey.

May your journey from here
be filled with love and dreams
achieved. We'll miss you.

What alarm clock I hear you ask?
Enjoy that!

Days of laughter and happiness is
what I wish for you. I'll miss you.

I'll miss the amazing perspective
on life you provide each day.

I'm going to miss your friendship.
I'm going to miss your expertise.
I'm going to miss.... You.

A happy day for you,
sad day for me. I'll miss you.

21 Special Birthdays

(18, 21, etc)

Congratulations on reaching (18/21/XX) Have a wonderful and memorable day.

•••••••

This is such a special milestone that I wanted to let you know just how proud I/we are of you. A very special person indeed. Happy Birthday.

•••••••

Happy Birthday – please learn this phrase as fast as you can and say it with gusto - "stop treating me like a kid!"

•••••••

I think it's time to paint the town whatever color you like. It's your dream, go for it.

•••••••

Wow! 18/21 huh? What exactly are you waiting for? Never wait or ask for permission to shine. HAPPY BIRTHDAY!!!

May your first official year as an adult be simply amazing. Starting…. Now!

•••••••

A new Birthday, a new chapter, turn the page and start writing the words, your words. Congratulations.

•••••••

You deserve this day and all that comes with it because you make the world a better place. Happy Birthday and Congratulations.

•••••••

I've got the best seat in the house to watch all your dreams come true. I think it's going to be a great performance.

•••••••

You feel like you can take on the world. Go ahead, if not you, then who? Happy Birthday.

May the doors to opportunities open when you knock on them. If they don't – BANG on them!

* * * * * * * *

The journey has been great so far, now, take the shackles off and watch for amazing things to come.

* * * * * * * *

Remember that you'll never grow if you don't go beyond something you've already mastered. Enjoy each one of these very precious steps in your journey.

* * * * * * * *

The birthday you can't avoid, the growing up part is completely optional.
Happy Birthday.

* * * * * * * *

Today we celebrate YOU, just YOU, Special YOU, Unique YOU and of course... Wonderful YOU.
Happy Birthday to YOU.

May the sunshine of the day smile upon your face.

* * * * * * * *

The only time Success comes before Work is in the Dictionary – roll your sleeves up and grab life with the passion you have inside.

* * * * * * * *

You can only be young and immature for a short while before the young runs out.
Make the most of it!
Happy Birthday.

* * * * * * * *

Remember this Birthday well. For when you're 30 – you will be 18 forever with 12 years experience.

* * * * * * * *

Go ahead and make this Birthday like the others you're going to celebrate – Brilliant!

22 ⬥ Success Quotes

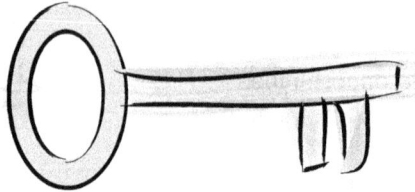

"Carpe Diem" - Seize The Day.

Be Decisive... Even If It Means
You'll Sometimes Be Wrong.

If an opportunity
presents itself - say YES...
then MAKE IT HAPPEN!!!!

Be Brave.
Even if you're not, pretend to be.
No one can tell the difference.

When ISN'T it the right time to do
the right thing?

When Was The Last
Time You Asked:
WHAT DO I WANT TO BE?

Your Worst Day Doing Something
You LOVE is Better Than....
Your Best Day Doing
Something You Hate!

Have good posture - Enter a room
with purpose and confidence.

Stop!
Breathe, Relax....
Breathe, Relax....
Continue for the next 5 minutes
and feel the difference!

Remember that Overnight
success usually takes
about 15 years!

Leave everything a little better than you found it.

EAT THE ELEPHANT – just one bite at a time.

Never underestimate your power to change yourself.

Spend Time To Dream - It's How Things Happen to YOU!

Kindness ALWAYS wins! Always, Always, Always!

Be the first to say HELLO.

Money will not make you successful - ULTIMATE happiness comes from within!

Say PLEASE and THANK YOU a LOT.

If you could live yesterday over again – what would you do different to make it more memorable?

The way you spend your time... in detail... illustrates EXACTLY what you care about.

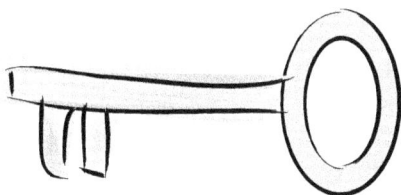

23 ◆ Sympathy

No words can describe
how you feel.
Know that you are surrounded
by many who care.

＊ ＊ ＊ ＊ ＊ ＊ ＊

I'll sit with you, cry with you
and hold your hand.
If you need me I'll be there.

＊ ＊ ＊ ＊ ＊ ＊ ＊

This hurt is very real,
I can share it with you,
Cry with you, Love You,
or just be there.

＊ ＊ ＊ ＊ ＊ ＊ ＊

My eyes burn with sorrow,
knowing I can't heal your pain
But know I'm always here for you.

＊ ＊ ＊ ＊ ＊ ＊ ＊

How lucky were we to have
known someone who was so
hard to say goodbye to.

Your tears honor the
one you loved.

＊ ＊ ＊ ＊ ＊ ＊ ＊

A life that brought us together
leaves us memories that
will never fade.

＊ ＊ ＊ ＊ ＊ ＊ ＊

The celebration of a life, is to
cherish memories of
many fine days.

＊ ＊ ＊ ＊ ＊ ＊ ＊

In our memories,
thoughts and dreams.
They live in our hearts,
in secret, untouchable places.
May the sun shine
warmly upon your face.
As you go on this journey
through loss.

＊ ＊ ＊ ＊ ＊ ＊ ＊

We cry because it's over, but we
should smile because it happened.

May warm thoughts and good
wishes surround you at this time.

We have arms so we can hug,
I'm saving many for you.

Deeply saddened, sincerest
thoughts, much love,
much strength.

Know that there are many who
will help you share the burden
of weight you feel on
your shoulders.

When you can't imagine life
without them, I'm here to talk
with you.

There's nothing better than a
friend in time of need.

Thinking of you, here for you,
heartfelt thoughts for you,
love for you.

On the thousands of times a day
you will remember them, call me.

May you and your family know
your wellbeing is being
prayed for at this time.

I'm here to listen when
you're ready.

24 Thank You

A heartfelt Thank You
just for being there.

* * * * * * *

It takes courage to say
what you said,
and for that I sincerely
Thank You.

* * * * * * *

Thank You for crossing
my path in life,
I am forever changed as a result.

* * * * * * *

Since our paths crossed
on this life journey,
my life has dramatically improved
– Thank You

* * * * * * *

I appreciate you being in this
world more than you know.

You're a shining star that lights
the way for others –
Thank You.

* * * * * * *

Thank you for showing me that
there are no shortcuts to a place
worth going to. You've made an
amazing difference in my life.

* * * * * * *

When I need you,
you're always there –
Thank You.

* * * * * * *

The flowers you sent
brightened up my day –
Thank You.

* * * * * * *

Thank you for being that special
friend we all dream about.

Thanks for taking time to see me –
I appreciate it.

Where did you learn to be so
caring, kind and thoughtful?
Thank You.

It's always great to stop, have a
conversation and catch up.
The precious things are
simple aren't they?
Thank You.

I am truly humbled by
all you have done.

Thank you for your Random Act
Of Kindness that touched me and
changed my life.

Your shoulder and your ears
helped me get through
a tough time –
Thank You.

You are a beautiful person
with much grace.
You were perfect for me –
thank you.

Your love touches me in more
ways than you could ever know.

My taste in friends sometimes
amazes even me!

A beautiful day is any
one that you're in.

25 Wedding Or Engagement

On The Day You Say "I Do",
May the world shine forever
upon both of you.

* * * * * * * *

May you love each other
more today than yesterday.
And more tomorrow than today.

* * * * * * * *

May the Angels of Love
fly over you forever.
As you begin this life together

* * * * * * * *

You've decided to join as
partners, on this journey
we call life.
This gift of love is priceless,
may you always feel this glow.

* * * * * * * *

A life together can be simple and
difficult all at once. The secret to
happiness is to Love one another.

"Happily Ever After"
Starts....Now!

* * * * * * * *

It's obvious when two people
are made for each other –
Congratulations.

* * * * * * * *

May your days be filled with joy,
your future filled with happiness
and may all your dreams
come true together.

* * * * * * * *

You've started the rest of
your lives together –
Congratulations.

* * * * * * * *

Wishing you a lifetime of love and
happiness together – sincerest
Congratulations.

May the tender loving moments
you share last the rest
of your lives.

Love is a whole of heart for a
whole of life experience.

Your happiness means so much to
us, we're thrilled about
your engagement.
Sincerest Congratulations.

May you fall in love with each
other many, many times.

To be in Love is to wipe out all
sense of time. Congratulations.

Your soul has no hiding place
when you're in love.

Just be happy and
Love one another.

May the celebration continue for
years to come following your
wedding day.
Congratulations.

Love is the ability to look in the
same direction as your partner.

The union of marriage is where
good forgivers unite.

About the Author...

Bruce Hultgren took a life changing event in his life in 1999 and turned it into a positive product that is now affecting millions around the world.

Following a professional basketball playing career in Australia – the 6'6" (198cm) Bruce is probably the last person walking down the street you'd expect to be the writer of these beautiful and moving words.

"It's a gift I uncovered during that moving time in my life, and now I've just run with it. Once I get the idea for a verse for an Angel – it may take a moment or a month to come out through my pen. But when it is ready to come out – I start writing – and many of these verses come out without errors – just as you see them on the cards." Says Bruce.

With a happy and sincere demeanor, a constant smile and an infectious enthusiasm for life and all things it brings – Bruce can be seen sharing this enthusiasm and positiveness throughout his daily writings of his "Life Tips" (see and become a fan (like) on Facebook www.facebook.com/pocketangels) and coaching kids in basketball, life and sport.

An accomplished speaker with a positive message, much experience in business and in life – with a history and discipline of sport, business and travel around the world – his talks can focus on many different areas.

Yet – if you ask Bruce what his greatest life achievement is to date – he will instantly praise his beautiful wife Belinda and his boys Conner and Jamieson. (yes – they're going to be very tall as well!)

That's Bruce Hultgren... so far!!!

A Daughter Is An Angel

To a very special Angel
Who brightens up our day

With just your smile or twinkling eyes
You glow in every way

So keep this Angel by your side
To remember someone cares

This Angel will keep you safe and sound
Love surrounds you... everywhere

www.pocketangels.co.uk   B. Hultgren

Guardian Pocket Angel

I am a Guardian Angel
To give you guidance, strength and love

I will wrap my wings around you
Feel them now, soft like a dove

You are cared for by many
Who carry you in their thoughts

So hold me tight when you feel the need
Everything... will be alright

B. Hultgren   www.pocketangels.com

If You Went Away...

The days...
They would be hollow

The sun may as well not shine
And although you may not know it
I smile when you come to mind

The little things you do
A simple gesture true

The world is simply a better place
And that's because of YOU

www.pocketangels.com

B. Hultgren

Sympathy Angel

No words or hugs can help you
To describe just how you feel

The sense of loss, the heartache
And oh... this hurt is real

But in the time
When you feel the need
Just hold this Angel tight

You are surrounded by abounding love
In time, it will be alright.

B.Hultgren   RIP Janet   www.pocketangels.com.au

www.ingramcontent.com/pod-product-compliance
Lightning Source LLC
Chambersburg PA
CBHW060643280326
41933CB00012B/2127